W9-AHZ-781

Creative Crafts for kids

Fabulous Fashion Crafts

Tracy Nelson Maurer

ROURKE PUBLISHING

Vero Beach, Florida 32964

www.rourkepublishing.com

Author Acknowledgments
Thank you to Meg, Tommy, Kim and the crews at Rourke and Blue Door.

Photo credits: All photos © Blue Door Publishing except: Cover © Marish, Ermakova Djamilia, Blue Door Publishing; Title Page © Marish, Ermakova Djamilia; Page 4 courtesy of The Library of Congress; Page 5 © Bobby Deal/RealDealPhoto, jackhollingsworthcom, MaszaS; Page 13 © Travis Manley

Editor: Meg Greve

Cover and page design by Nicola Stratford, Blue Door Publishing

Library of Congress Cataloging-in-Publication Data

Maurer, Tracy, 1965-
  Fabulous fashion crafts / Tracy Maurer.
    p. cm. -- (Creative crafts for kids)
  Includes index.
  ISBN 978-1-60694-341-0 (hard cover)
  ISBN 978-1-60694-503-2 (soft cover)
  1. Handicraft for girls--Juvenile literature. 2. Dress accessories--Juvenile literature. I. Title.
  TT171.M167 2009
  745.5--dc22
                                2009010699

Printed in the USA

www.rourkepublishing.com - rourke@rourkepublishing.com
Post Office Box 643328 Vero Beach, Florida 32964

contents

Fashion from Head to Toe

Styles change over time. Boys no longer wear short pants called knickers. Girls no longer wear **petticoats**. But fashion is more than popular clothing styles. **Accessories**, such as jewelry, hats, and shoes, give fashion its flair.

changing Styles

Opinions may change about certain styles over time. Until the 1970s, girls who wore denim jeans to school were often sent home by their teachers. Today most students wear jeans to school, and so do the teachers!

What's Your Style?

Are you dressy, sporty, or casual? Whatever style is your favorite, you don't have to spend a lot of money to look terrific. Start your own fashion **trends** from head to toe with the fun ideas in this book.

Starter Supplies

Gather these supplies in a box or bucket to keep them handy for your projects.

- craft glue
- glitter fabric paint
- permanent fabric glue
- plastic zipper bags
- scissors
- tape measure
- thin wire
- wire cutters

Starter Supplies

Find supplies for these projects at a craft store or around your home. Collect ribbons, beads, thin wire, yarn, buttons, broken jewelry, and extra pieces of fabric and felt for your fashion projects. Always ask for an adult's permission and help with cutting, pinning, or sewing.

If possible, label a new pair of scissors just for fabric. Using them on paper will dull the blades and tear fabric.

FABRIC

Beaded Bobby Pin

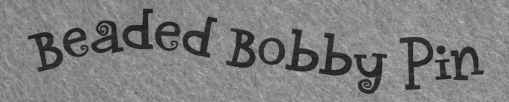

You Will need:

- 1 bobby pin
- 6 inches (15 centimeters) of thin, 26-gauge silver wire
- wire cutter
- beads

T i P

Create a pattern with your beads. To test your pattern, slip the beads onto an extra strip of wire. Hold this wire against your bobby pin. Does your pattern fit on the bobby pin?

Fashion covers you from head to toe. Hair accessories top the list. This project uses a bobby pin and beads. For different styles, try adding silk flowers, bows, or feathery trim to barrettes, headbands, combs, and elastic bands.

Here's How:

1. Make a 1/2-inch (1.25 centimeters) hook at the bottom of the wire. It should look like a J.

2. Hook the curved end of the bobby pin. Twist the short wire tail around the base of the long wire.

3. Bend the remaining wire so it stands straight. Thread one bead onto the wire. Hold the bead snug to the bobby pin's shorter top arm. Wrap the wire around just the top arm.

4. Bend the wire upright again. Repeat with a second bead. Again, hold the bead snug to the bobby pin's arm and wrap the wire. Continue until no more beads will fit on the arm.

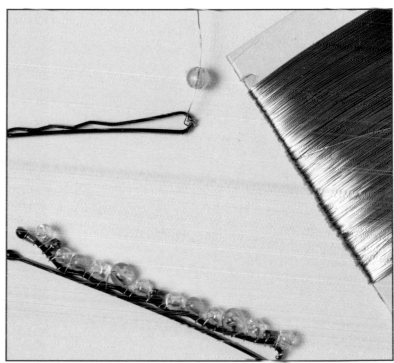

5. Finish by twisting the remaining wire tightly around the end of the top arm at least two times. Snip off extra wire.

More Hair Jewelry

Here are a few more ideas for your hair fashions.

- Make beaded dangles. Cut a 6-inch (15-centimeter) wire strip and bend in half. Thread beads onto the wire. Twist the ends around the closed end of a bobby pin or barrette.
- Add glitter fabric paint to the tips of silk flowers. Cut off the plastic stems. Glue the flowers to a barrette or headband. Use fabric strips with sticky backs to attach silk flowers to elastic bands.
- Cut 20 strips of thin ribbon, each 4 inches (10 centimeters) long. Wrap each strip around the top arm of a barrette and tie in a knot. Scrunch as many ribbons onto the barrette as you can.

Angel necklace

Who knew that paper clips could look so pretty? Choose beads, ribbon, and a **ribbon rose** in your favorite color, or choose one in your friend's **birthstone**. This project also makes a pretty Christmas tree ornament in any color.

Here's How:

1. Fold the ribbon in half, making a long U. Slip the U under the back of the clip and around to the front. Pull the two long ends through the loop. Pull the long ends to tighten the loop to the clip.

2. Slip the bead for the angel's head onto the two long ends. With the two long ends, tie two knots on top of the bead.

3. Slip four or five beads for each wing onto each of the **crisscrossed** paper clip wires and push into place. Ask an adult to help you lift the wire.

4. Dab glue under the bead for the angel's head and on the fronts of the crisscrossed wires. Center the ribbon rose in the glue over the crisscrossed ends. Let it dry overnight.

5. Tie a knot in the long ribbon ends to make the necklace.

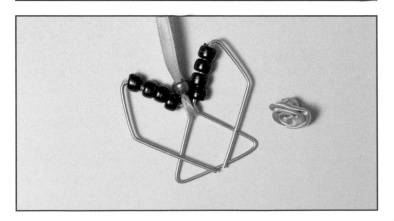

Birthstone chart

Month	Name of Birthstone	Color of Birthstone
January	garnet	deep red
February	amethyst	purple
March	aquamarine	light blue
April	diamond	white
May	emerald	green
June	pearl	creamy white
July	ruby	red
August	peridot	lime green
September	sapphire	deep blue
October	opal	pink
November	citrine	yellow
December	blue topaz	blue

TiP

Instead of an angel, make a butterfly by putting beads all the way around the paper clip before you put the ribbon on. String a black bead on the ribbons for the head. Use a pipe cleaner in the middle for the body and antennae.

You Will need:

- tape measure
- scissors
- 1.5 yard (1.4 meters) each of three patterned 1/2-inch (1.25 centimeter) grosgrain ribbons and two 1/8-inch (.63-centimeter) satin ribbons, all in similar colors
- 2 large, 1-inch (2.5-centimeter) beads with wide holes

Ribbon Belt

Fabric belts never go out of style. This ribbon belt project lets you mix and match ribbons for unique fashions.

Here's How:

1. Stretch all the ribbons out, side by side. Loop all of the ribbons together around four fingers of one hand. Then pull the tails through the loop to make an **overhand knot** about 6 inches (15.25 centimeters) from the end.

2. Slip a large bead over all of the ribbons. Snug it up to your overhand knot. Tie another overhand knot just below the bead.

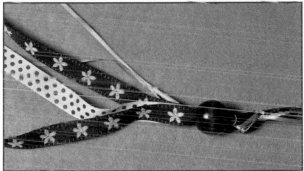

3. Repeat the knots and bead on the other end.

4. Cover your work area. Apply clear fabric glue on the ends of each ribbon. This helps prevent them from fraying. Allow the glue to dry overnight.

5. Thread your belt through your belt loops and tie a loose knot. Let the ribbon ends dangle.

For special holidays, such as the Fourth of July or Halloween, make a belt using the colors that symbolize that holiday. You can even make a noisy belt by attaching jingle bells instead of beads!

You Will need:

- denim jeans, one leg with hem at the bottom
- scissors
- sewing needle
- thread
- 1 yard (.91 meter) of 1-inch (2.5-centimeter) wide grosgrain ribbon
- 6-inch (15-centimeter) strip of hook-and-loop fasteners with sticky back closures
- decorations such as **appliqués**, fancy ribbons, or fabric paint

16

denim Purse

When your favorite jeans wear out, save them for your craft box. Many craft projects like this one use the denim from jeans. Start with this easy project and then invent your own denim crafts! Be sure to ask your parent's permission before you start this project.

Here's How:

1. Measure 10 inches (25 centimeters) from the bottom **hem** of the jean leg toward the knee. Cut across the leg. Save the remaining denim for other crafts.

2. Cut about 18 inches (46 centimeters) of thread from the **spool**. Slip one end of the thread through the eye of the needle and pull half of the thread through. Line up the ends evenly and tie a knot. Tie another knot on top of the first knot.

3. Turn the leg inside out and smooth the fabric. Starting about 1/2 inch (1.25 centimeters) in from the rough end that you just cut, sew a backstitch (see page 19) across the width of the leg. Be sure to poke your needle through both layers of denim. Tie a knot in the thread next to the denim when you finish. Snip the thread just below the needle to release it.

10 inches (25 centimeters)

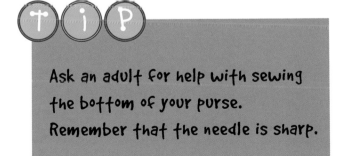

Ask an adult for help with sewing the bottom of your purse. Remember that the needle is sharp.

17

4. Turn the denim so it is no longer inside out. The hemmed edge is now the top. The part you sewed is now the bottom.

5. Just below the hem and next to each seam, fold the denim. Snip a 1/2-inch (1.25 centimeter) sideways slit into the fold, not cutting into the seam or hem.

6. Starting from inside the purse, poke one end of the ribbon through a slit. Pull about 3 inches (7.5 centimeters) of ribbon through the hole. Tie and knot the short end to the long ribbon that is now the purse strap. Repeat with the other slit.

7. Keep the two hook-and-loop strips attached for now. Peel the tape from one hook-and-loop strip. Stick the strip sideways, inside the purse and just below the front hem. Peel the remaining tape. Press this strip onto the inside denim just below the back hem.

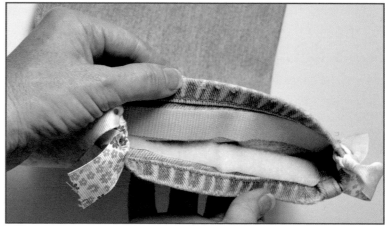

8. Decorate the purse with appliqués, ribbon, fabric paint, or other trim.

Learn The Backstitch

The backstitch makes a strong seam with small, even stitches. Many crafts call for this stitch. It also comes in handy for mending clothes.

1. Thread the needle and knot the ends. Poke the point of the needle down through both layers of fabric. Hold the needle and pull gently until the knot at the end of the thread catches on the top fabric.

2. Move the needle point over about 1/2 inch (1.25 centimeters) on the back side of the fabric. Poke it up through both layers of fabric. Hold the needle and pull gently until all the thread pulls through.

3. Poke the needle down about 1/4 inch (.6 centimeter) back from where it just came up. Tug gently until all the thread pulls through.

4. Repeat steps 2 and 3, moving one long stitch forward and one half stitch back. Keep your stitches in a straight line. Also, avoid tugging too hard on the thread or the fabric will bunch.

5. To finish, knot the thread close to the fabric twice. To make a tighter knot, make a small stitch in the fabric near the end of your stitching. Then pass the needle twice through the loop of thread before pulling it tight. Snip the thread and put your needle in a safe place.

You Will Need:

- clean, dry T-shirt in a light color
- colorful permanent markers or fabric markers

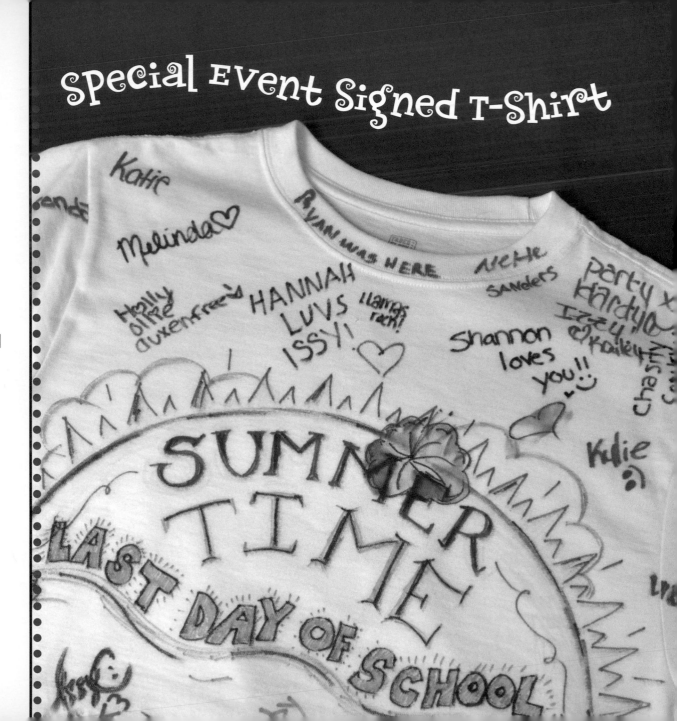

Special Event Signed T-Shirt

Make a special event even more memorable with a T-shirt signed by your friends. Wear the shirt and ask friends to use colorful permanent markers to autograph your shirt!

Here's How:

1. Using the permanent markers or fabric markers, write the name of the event on the front or back. Include the date. Draw pictures that represent the event. For example, draw a picture of a basketball for a special basketball game or tents and a campfire for summer camp.

2. Keep several permanent markers handy for friends to use. Be sure to ask your coach, teacher, or other leader to sign your shirt, too.

Here are some special occasions for making a signed T-shirt.

- sleepover or birthday party – let everyone make a shirt to take home
- last game of your team's season
- cast party for plays or musicals
- class field trip or last day of school
- club projects, such as Girl or Boy Scouts, 4-H, or Boys & Girls club

Signed T-Shirt Group Photo Option

This project looks terrific with or without the group picture. If you choose to add a photo, ask a parent to help with these items:

- digital camera
- color inkjet printer
- iron-on transfer paper
- iron and ironing board

1. Ask a parent to take a digital picture of you and your group.

2. With your parent's help, print out the picture using a color inkjet printer with iron-on transfer paper for each shirt. Ask to have the image ironed onto your shirt.

Splashy Socks

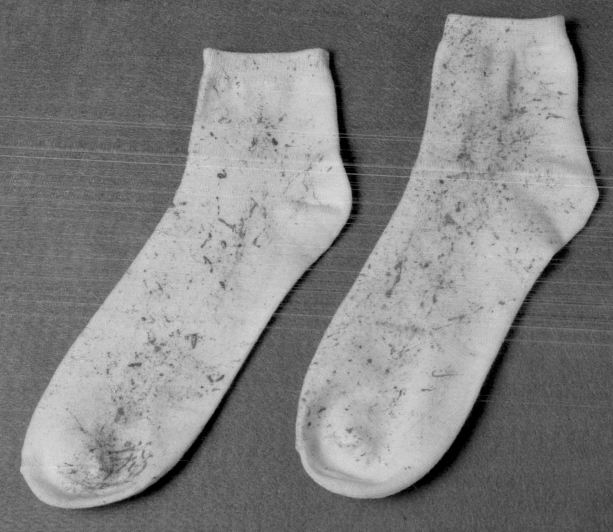

23

Colorful socks bring your outfits together. Make these socks in colors to match your favorite clothing or make a new outfit by splashing a T-shirt, too.

Here's How:

1. Cover your work area with lots of newspapers. This is a very messy project.

2. Turn the cardboard box on its side, so the opening is facing you.

3. Crumple a sheet of wax paper or a used grocery bag and stuff it into a sock. This stretches the fabric as if your foot was inside the sock. Repeat with the second sock.

4. Put the socks in the box to work on them.

5. Pour a small pool of fabric paint on a paper plate. Tap your toothbrush bristles in the paint to pick up a thin layer of paint.

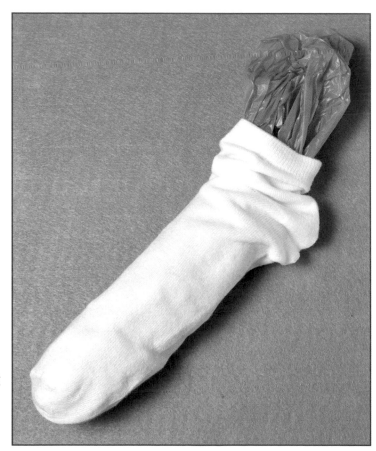

6. Use your fingers to flick the paint at the socks. Splash the paint on all parts of the socks. Repeat with other colors. Try not to touch the socks or the splashes will smear.

7. Clean up your work area. Allow your socks to dry overnight in the box.

Dress Up Your Socks

Paint patterns such as polka dots or write your name with fabric paint on your sock. Stitch or use permanent fabric glue to attach a small ribbon bow to the side of sock. You can also attach premade appliqués, sparkly buttons, or pom-poms around the opening of the socks.

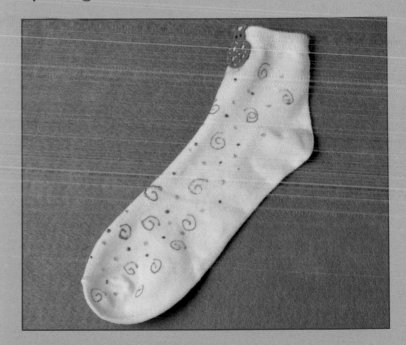

Sporty Shoelaces

Show your team spirit all the way down to your toes. Make enough shoelaces for your entire team or cheerleading squad, too.

Here's How:

1. Cover your work area.

2. Stretch the shoelaces over the cardboard. Pin each end into the cardboard. Tape the plastic shoelace tips to avoid painting them.

3. Paint a pattern on each shoelace. Let the shoelaces dry. Use the markers to fill in spaces or to write words.

4. Turn the shoelaces over. Pin them again. Paint the other side. Let the shoelaces dry. Finish with the markers. Remove the tape over the tips.

Pattern ideas

Try different patterns on your shoelaces. Here are some ideas:
- dots, big and small, close or far apart
- blocks of color next to each other
- write your name or words, such as Go Team!
- wavy lines or curly squiggles
- shapes, such as triangles, diamonds, or squares
- smiley faces made with markers on top of dry yellow paint dots

You will Need:

- one pair of flip-flops in your size
- 30 fabric pieces cut to 1 x 6 inch (2.5 x 15 centimeter) strips
- scissors

Try polar fleece fabric for cozy flip-flops, use satin ribbon strips for fancy flip-flops, or knitting yarn for fluffy flip-flops.

Fluffy Flip-flops

fleece

knitting yarn

Give an ordinary pair of plastic flip-flops a trendy look in minutes. You will want to make a pair to match every summer outfit!

Here's How:

1. Cut fabric strips. If fabric ends fray, seal the ends with a thin layer of clear fabric glue and allow them to dry before attaching to flip-flops.

2. Tie 15 strips onto the straps of one sandal using a single knot for each strip. Use more or less strips, depending on the type of fabric and how full it looks. Fluff them when you finish.

3. Repeat for the second flip-flop.

Try More Styles

Tap your imagination to create more flip-flop styles. Here are some ideas.

- Glue buttons or swirl glitter fabric paint onto the straps.
- Glue feather trim along the tops of the straps.
- Remove the plastic stems from two large daisy silk flowers. Glue a flower to the center V of each strap.

To Wear or to Share

Wear your fashions with pride. Make several of your favorite projects for your friends, too. Or, invite your friends to make their own projects with you! Once you start making fashion crafts, you will find all kinds of clothing and accessories ready for your special style.

Update an old bracelet with strips of ribbon, glitter glue, or sparkly stickers.

Glossary

accessories (ak-SESS-uh-reez): items worn to match the clothing

appliqués (ap-luh-KAYZ): stitched decorations for fabric

birthstone (BURTH-stone): the gem or other special stone that means the month when a person was born

crisscrossed (KRISS-krawssd): lines that have crossed like an X

gauge (GAJE): a measurement of a wire's thickness

hem (HEM): the end of a shirt or pants that is folded over and sewn closed

opinions (uh-PIN-yuhnz): ideas or beliefs

overhand knot (OH-vur-hand nawt): a simple knot made with a loop over the hand

petticoats (PET-ee-kotes): thin slips worn under skirts or dresses

ribbon rose (RIB-uhn ROZE): a flower design made from a ribbon that is ready to attach to fabric

spool (SPOOL): a small cylinder or reel that holds thread

trends (TRENDZ): styles of dress that are popular for short periods of time

index

Websites to Visit

crafts.suite101.com/general

familyfun.go.com/arts-and-crafts/

www.kaboose.com/

kids.nationalgeographic.com/Activities/Crafts

About The Author

Tracy Nelson Maurer has written more than 60 fiction and nonfiction books for children. She loved crafts as a child and she still likes to take the scissors for a whirl. Tracy lives near Minneapolis, Minnesota, with her husband and two children.